My Journey Around the World

Jeremy Bear

OXFORD
UNIVERSITY PRESS

OXFORD
UNIVERSITY PRESS

Great Clarendon Street, Oxford, OX2 6DP

Oxford University Press is a department of the University of Oxford.
It furthers the University's objective of excellence in research, scholarship,
and education by publishing worldwide in

Oxford New York

Auckland Bangkok Buenos Aires Cape Town Chennai
Dar es Salaam Delhi Hong Kong Istanbul Karachi Kolkata
Kuala Lumpur Madrid Melbourne Mexico City Mumbai
Nairobi São Paulo Shanghai Taipei Tokyo Toronto

Oxford is a registered trade mark of Oxford University Press
in the UK and in certain other countries

Text © Alison Morris 1999

The moral rights of the author have been asserted

Database right Oxford University Press (maker)

First published by Oxford University Press 1999
10 9 8 7 6 5 4

All rights reserved. No part of this publication may be reproduced,
stored in a retrieval system, or transmitted, in any form or by any means,
without the prior permission in writing of Oxford University Press, or as
expressly permitted by law, or under terms agreed with the appropriate
reprographics rights organization. Enquiries concerning reproduction
outside the scope of the above should be sent to the Rights Department,
Oxford University Press, at the address above

You must not circulate this book in any other binding or cover
and you must impose this same condition on any acquirer

A CIP record for this book is available from the British Library

ISBN 0 19 915593 3
Available in packs
Toys Pack of Six   (one of each book)   ISBN 0 19 915595 X
Toys Class Pack   (six of each book)   ISBN 0 19 915617 4

Printed in China

Acknowledgements

The publisher would like to thank the following for permission
to reproduce photographs:

Ace Photo Library pp 12, 15 (*top*), 16; Corbis UK p 8; Hutchison Library
p 17; J. Allan Cash pp 6, 7, 9, 12 (*top*), 15; Planet Earth p 11; Telegraph
Colour Library p 8 (*left*), 11 (*left*); Traders Hotel, Singapore p 10.

All other photography by Martin Sookias.

Maps by Peter Bull Art Studio.

With special thanks to the children and staff of St Bartholomew's School,
Wootton Bassett, and St Barnabas School, Oxford, for their assistance.

Contents

Getting ready 4
United States of America ... 6
New Zealand 8
Singapore 10
Maldive Islands 12
Isle of Wight 14
Kenya 16
Wootton Bassett 18
Working with Class 2M 20
My journey around
    the world 22
Index 24

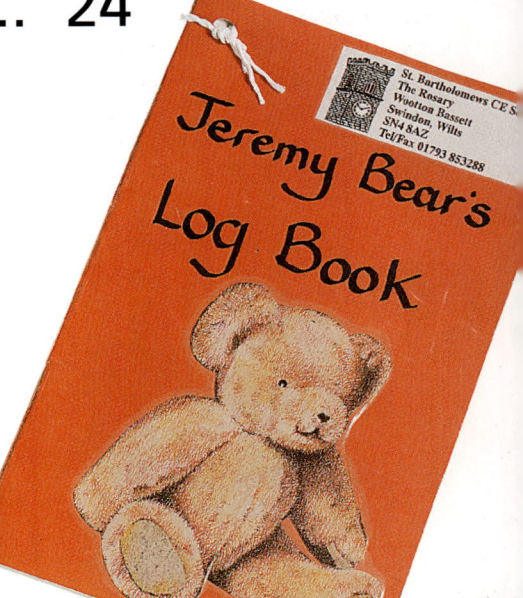

Getting ready

January 20th 1996

Name: Jeremy Bear
Address: St Bartholomew's School, Wootton Bassett, UK
Reason for journey: to help Mrs Morris and Class 2M with their project on journeys. They wanted to find out about other countries.

I went on a journey around the world. This book records my trip.

Thomas and Joshua told us that their fathers were going to America. They said I could go too.

I took lots of things with me. ▼

I went to Heathrow airport. I was very excited.

USA

January 21st 1996

I flew to the United States. The flight took about 8 hours.

I sat with the pilot in the cockpit.

I had some American dollars to spend.

United States of America

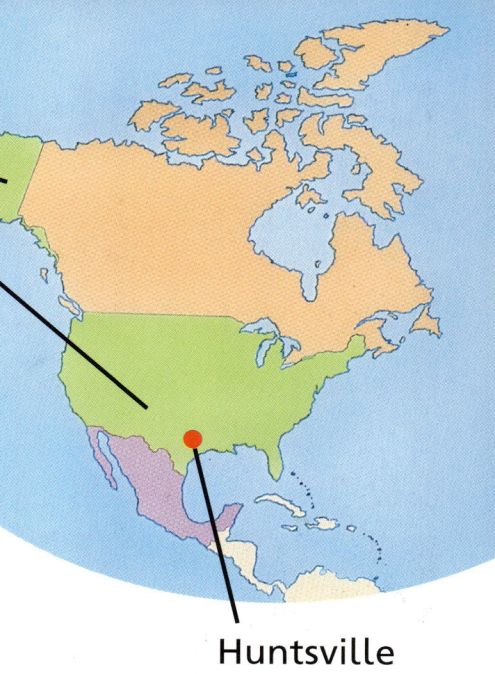

I visited the Space Shuttle. I found out that the Space Shuttle had two rockets to send it into space, and it could take seven crew.

Huntsville

I bought a badge for a dollar. ▼

I wish that I could go on a journey into space.

New Zealand

January 27th 1996

Next, I flew to New Zealand. I went on a cruise, and I helped the Captain steer the boat.

There are two islands in New Zealand. I went fishing near the North Island.

I caught this marlin.

I visited Russell School in the Bay of Islands. The children gave me a leather tie to wear around my neck.

I visited Auckland, on the North Island.

Singapore

February 15th 1996

I went to Singapore and I stayed at Traders Hotel.

This banner was outside the hotel. ▼

Traders Hotel Singapore Welcomes Jeremy Bear!!!

The Manager gave me an envelope with money inside. Envelopes like these are given to children at Chinese New Year.

I went to see a big statue called the Merlion.

Then I went to a rainforest. The weather was very hot and wet.

Maldive Islands

February 17th 1996

Next, I went to the Maldive Islands in the Indian Ocean.

▼ I went for a flight in a helicopter.

There are over 1000 Maldive Islands.

◄ The islands looked very small from the window.

I went to the beach.
It was very hot, and
the sea was very blue.

Maldive Islands

◀ I sat in the shade under a parasol but I still needed my sun cream.

13

Isle of Wight

February 27th 1996

Next, I went to the Isle of Wight in the UK. I visited Fiveways School in Ryde.

The children gave me a wooden medal to wear.

I sent this fax to Class 2M

I went on a hovercraft to Southampton.

Then I went in a car to Heathrow airport in London.

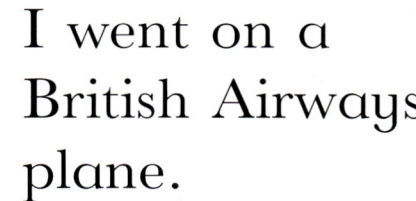

I went on a British Airways plane.

Kenya

March 5th 1996

I flew to Kenya next. Kenya is a country in Africa.

I went to visit an elephant orphanage. Baby elephants go there when their parents die.

I went to Nairobi, the capital of Kenya. There were lots of baskets and wooden animals on the market stalls.

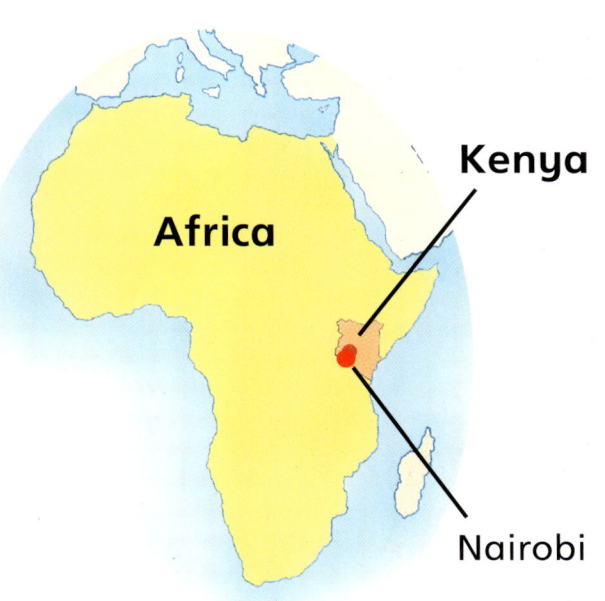

I bought a wooden necklace. ▶

Wootton Bassett

March 13th 1996

I got back to St Bartholomew's School.
Mrs Morris and Class 2M were very pleased to see me.

The children read about the places I had visited. They followed my journey on the globe.

I collected lots of things on my journey.

I had lots of plane tickets.

I had money from five countries. Money is called currency.

Working with Class 2M

The children found out a lot about other countries.

They drew my journey on a map of the world and put it on the wall.

◀ They wrote letters to everyone who had helped me.

They drew pictures of me.
▼

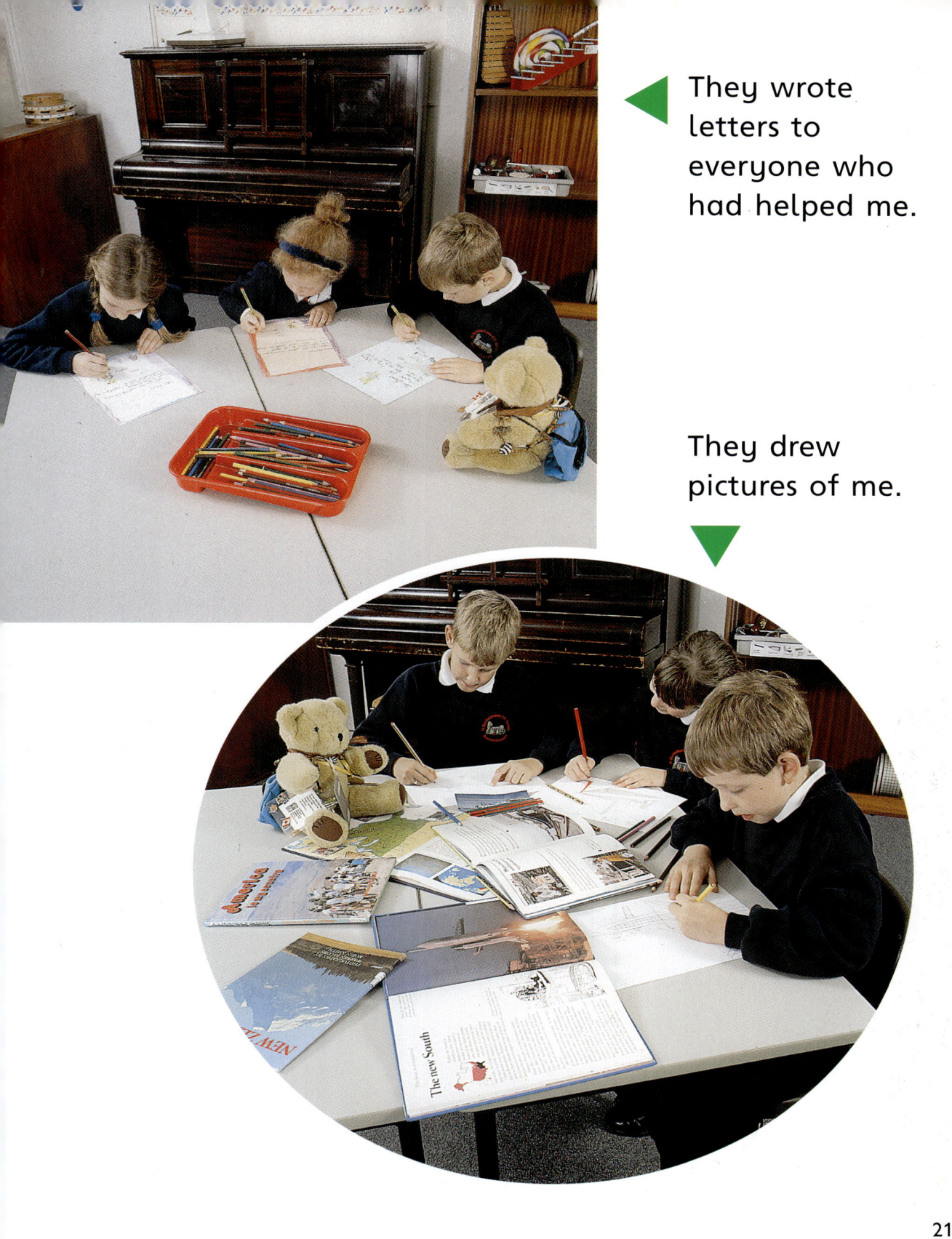

My journey around the world

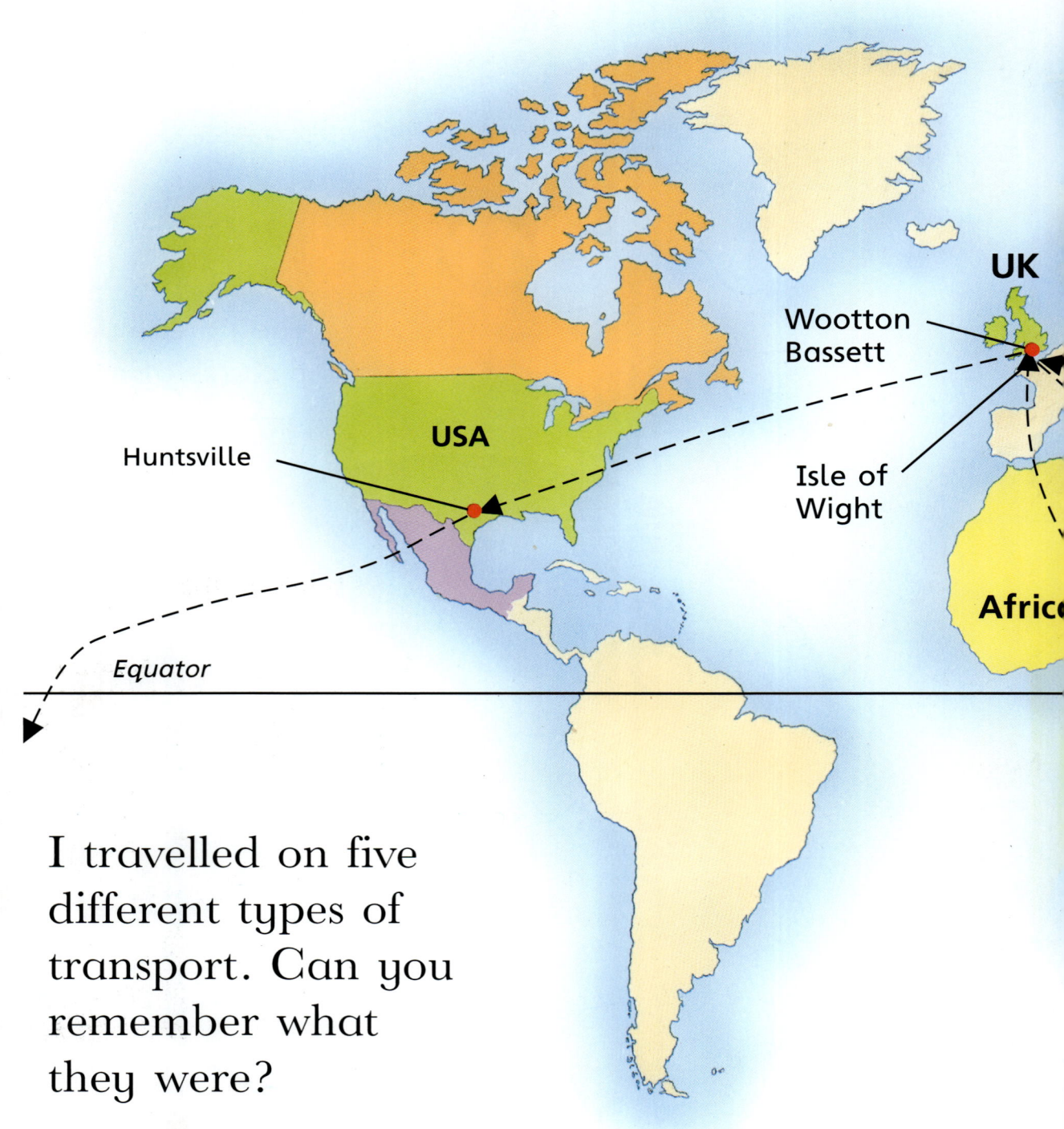

I travelled on five different types of transport. Can you remember what they were?

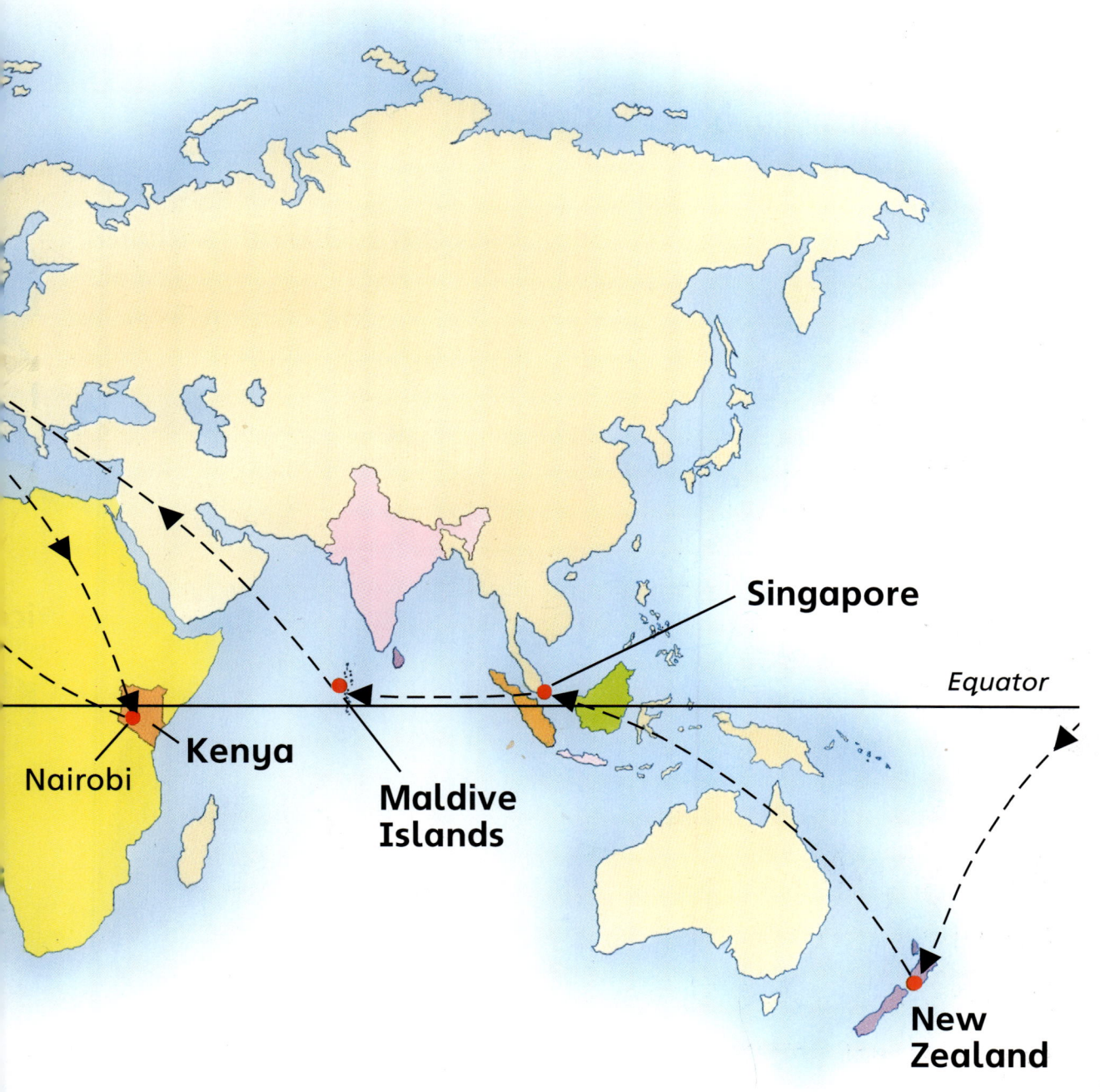

a b c d e f g h i j k l m n o p q r s t u v w x y z

Index

banner   10
boat   8
Chinese New Year   10
cockpit   6
elephants   16
fax   14
helicopter   12
hovercraft   15
market   17
marlin   8
medal   14
money   10, 19
necklace   17
pilot   6
plane   15
space shuttle   7

Goodbye! Safe journeys always.

24